LIVING IN... BRAZIL

by Chloe Perkins
illustrated by Tom Woolley

READY-TO-READ

SIMON SPOTLIGHT

An imprint of Simon & Schuster Children's Publishing Division • New York   London   Toronto   Sydney   New Delhi • 1230 Avenue of the Americas, New York, New York 10020 • This Simon Spotlight edition September 2017 • Text copyright © 2016 by Simon & Schuster, Inc. Illustrations copyright © 2016 by Tom Woolley • Additional artwork by Reg Silva
SIMON SPOTLIGHT, READY-TO-READ, and colophon are registered trademarks of Simon & Schuster, Inc. For information about special discounts for bulk purchases, please contact Simon & Schuster Special Sales at 1-866-506-1949 or business@simonandschuster.com.
Manufactured in China 0118 SDI

GLOSSARY

Border: an imaginary line that separates one country from another

Coastline: any place where a body of water meets land

Highlands: an area that contains many hills, mountains, and land that is high above the ground

Illegal: anything not allowed by the laws of a country

Mangrove: a group of bushes or trees with thick roots

Native Brazilian: a person who was, or whose ancestors were, living in Brazil before European explorers arrived in 1500 CE; native Brazilians come from many different tribes and ethnic groups, each of which has its own culture, customs, and beliefs

Rain Forest: a type of forest that takes in a lot of rain and has many trees and plants that grow very close together

Settler: a person who leaves their home to live in a new place, usually to create a colony, or community, for his or her people

Slavery: a practice in which a person can own another person and force him or her to work for free against their will

Tradition: something, such as a belief or practice, that has been passed down within a group for a long time

Tribe: a group of people who share the same language and culture

World Cup: an international soccer competition between countries that takes place each year

NOTE TO READERS: Some of these words may have more than one definition. The definitions above are how these words are used in this book.

Oi! (say: oy)
That means "hi" in Portuguese.
My name is Marco, and
I live in Brazil.
Brazil is a country in
South America
where more than
two hundred million people live . . .
including me!

Brazil is the biggest
country in South America.
It borders every
South American country
except Chile and Ecuador.

VENEZUELA

GUYANA

COLOMBIA

SURINAME

FRENCH
GUIANA

ECUADOR

BRAZIL

PERU

BOLIVIA

PARAGUAY

CHILE

URUGUAY

ARGENTINA

Brazil has many
rivers, mountains,
and rain forests.
In fact, the natural wonders
of Brazil are what I love
most about my country!

In the north, the
Amazon rain forest
grows around the Amazon River.
The rain forest covers
nearly half of Brazil's land.
It is filled with many different
kinds of plants and animals,
from orchid flowers to jaguars!

Many tribes of native Brazilians
also live in the rain forest.
Because the rain forest is
home to people, plants,
and animals, Brazil has special
rules about the rain forest.
These rules protect it
from being destroyed.

In the south and center of Brazil are the Brazilian Highlands. They are called highlands because there are many mountains and hills there. There are lots of big cities in the highlands.

There are also lots of
cities along Brazil's coast.
Brazil has one of the longest
coastlines in the world.
People come from all
over to visit Brazil's
famous beaches!

RIO DE JANEIRO

Brazil has a lot of famous cities! Rio de Janeiro is home to the world's biggest Carnival. Carnival is a five-day celebration with parades, fancy costumes, and big parties. Brasília is our capital city. The whole city was built in four years!

BRASÍLIA

São Paulo is the biggest city
in Brazil. More than
twenty million people live there!
Manaus is a much smaller
city located in the north,
in the Amazon rain forest.

I live in a city on the beach called Recife (say: HEY-SEE-fee). My mom, sister, and I live in an apartment building in the center of the city.

RECIFE

My mom is a nurse at
the hospital.
She helps sick people
feel better.

My older sister works at a
bakery on our street.
She brings home extra
bread and cake every night.

Each morning my sister
and I eat breakfast together.
We munch on cheesy bread.
My mom works really
late at the hospital.
She's still sleeping
at breakfast time.

My sister walks me to school
on her way to work.
I go to a private school.
There are thirty kids
in my class.
We all wear the
same uniform.

School is very important
in Brazil. I have to study
hard so I can get a
good job someday.

Some kids in Brazil
don't finish school.
They have to work to
help their families.

In Brazil the school year goes
from February to December.
I have summer vacation
in January!

During the school year I learn
about math, reading, science,
and history. This morning we're
learning about Brazil's history.

Remember the native Brazilians?
Our history begins with
them. Native Brazilians
have lived here for at least
eleven thousand years!
Many of them practice
the same traditions they
did hundreds of years ago.

In 1500 the Portuguese explorer Pedro Cabral landed on the Brazilian coast. He claimed the land for Portugal. Settlers began moving here from Portugal and the rest of Europe.

Soon after, the settlers enslaved the native Brazilians and brought in more slaves from Africa. They forced them to work on big farms growing food. Many slaves fought to be free. Still, as time passed and Brazil grew, so did slavery.

But in 1822 the prince of Portugal
was given control of Brazil.
He declared that Brazil was
free to be its own country.
And in 1888 the prince's
granddaughter signed a law
that made slavery illegal.
The slaves were free!

After our history lesson,
it's time for science!
We are learning
about mangroves.
A mangrove is a group
of bushes or trees
with thick roots.

Mangroves are very important.
Their roots prevent sand
from being washed away
by the ocean.
And guess what?
Next week we're going on
a field trip to visit the
mangroves outside of Recife!

School ends at noon every day.
Lunch is an important meal
in Brazil, so many kids
eat at home with their families.
But my mom is still resting,
and my sister is at work,
so I eat lunch at school.
Today we're eating rice
and beans with fish.

I eat with my
best friend, Davi.
My favorite part of lunch
is the fresh pineapple juice.
It's so tasty!

Davi's dad picks us up
on his way home from work.
We all walk to Davi's house.
We change out of our
school uniforms and
play soccer with
the kids on Davi's street.

In Brazil soccer is very popular.
And it's no wonder:
Brazil has had some of the
best soccer players in the world!
My favorite is Pelé.
He helped Brazil win three
World Cups between 1958 and 1970!

We're really tired
after the game!
We snack on fruit
and start our homework.
We're writing a report
about mangroves.

My mom picks me up
from Davi's house
a few hours later.
At home I work
on my chores.
Then I watch some TV
until my sister gets home.

In Brazil we eat dinner very late—around nine o'clock! I set the table while my sister cooks. Tonight we're eating a stew made from beans, vegetables, and sausage, served over rice. Yum!

My mom tucks me in, and then
she leaves for work.
Before bed I like to read
stories about people in
other countries.
It would be so much fun
to travel around the world!
Would you like to visit
Brazil someday?

ALL ABOUT
BRAZIL!

NAME: Federative Republic of Brazil (Or Brazil for short!)

POPULATION: 204 million

CAPITAL: Brasília

LANGUAGE: Portuguese (Spanish, German, and tribal languages are commonly spoken in several regions)

TOTAL AREA: 3,287,612 square miles

GOVERNMENT: democracy, federal republic

CURRENCY: real (say: hey-AL)

FUN FACT: Most of Brazil (including Marco's home) is on the southern half of the Earth, so Marco has summer in January! When the southern half of the Earth is tilted toward the sun, it's summer. But at the same time, the northern half is tilted away from the sun and has winter.

FLAG: Green with a yellow diamond in the center. On the diamond is a blue circle with twenty-seven stars (twenty-six for each state, one for the capital). A white band says "ORDEM E PROGRESSO," which means "Order and Progress" in Portuguese.